FRANS HALS

ABOUT THE AUTHOR

Dr. Willem Beeren is a keeper at the Municipal Museum in
The Hague, and editor of the "Museumjournal", a periodical
which covers the activities of the museums of modern art in
Holland. Recently he published "Beeldverhaal", a book on
art of our time.

DR. WILLEM BEEREN

Frans Hals

BARNES & NOBLE, INC.

NEW YORK

Publishers • Booksellers • Since 1873

Editor: Anthony Bosman
Translation: Albert J. Fransella
Lay-out: Wim van Stek and Aart Verhoeven
Published in the United States in 1963
by Barnes & Noble, Inc., 105 Fifth Avenue, New York 3, N.Y.
© 1962 and printed in Holland by The Ysel Press Ltd, Deventer

Hals and His Times

Broad, dark landscapes, the subtle silhouettes of little towns around three or four large churches, interiors of incomparable simplicity and nobility, vast spaces inside church edifices, dramatic sailing ships on turbulent waters, bucolic scenes, tavern pictures of a haunting realism, the countless faces of profoundly serious men and women, lifelike group portraits, and the statuesque silence of the still lifes—how endlessly varied was Dutch painting in the seventeenth century! Sentiment itself was by no means constant, ranging as it did from the desolate melancholy of Hercules Seghers to the exuberance of Frans Hals. It is indeed difficult to deal collectively with such a gamut of emotions and such a diversity of subjects, though perhaps one general characteristic does stand out: the concentration upon comprehensive pictures, and the intense focus upon a few persons and things and their relationships. It is as if a huge storm of visions of Italian art had been lying over the coast of Holland and had now ascended to vanish into a heavenly sky full of angels.

Matter-of-fact Holland was telling its painters to utilize their eyes more in future, thus imposing a fresh duty upon the senses. This meant the end of fixed structures, of meticulous modelling, of tortured compositions, of obtrusive pathos, of directed anatomy, of perspective receding into a pin's head. From then on, the artist was to observe nature and animals, without needing the alibi of a Biblical or mythological scene. In a country where the horizon is so low above flat lowlands, he was to paint the enormous sky filled with greyish clouds in a dramatic light.

And just as intently the painter began to observe people. At a time when the Church no longer gave commissions to painters, and the State too was very sparing with them, there were many orders for portraits that satisfied the conceit of the middle classes and served to indicate the prosperity they had achieved. For all that, the perceptive artist was able to retain his tranquil outlook and to keep in step with the qualities of a people who had conducted their earthly affairs successfully and had drawn from the Bible, not religious fantasies, but a practical morality. That businesslike directive to painters to see things clearly was duly carried out; happily it did not prevent the artists from weaving their poetry into their skills. For in no other country in the world has the painter so well understood the marvellous art of being able to conjure—out of the most ordinary and seemingly obvious situations—those magic moments, those wonderful emotional depths, and reveal them for all posterity to enjoy.

Frans Hals both contradicts and confirms this picture of Dutch art. Stillness and poetry are strangers to him, but when we examine his work—that procession of merry, vivacious people set before us in all their undeniable lifelikeness—we can clearly detect in his astonishingly direct style the imprint of the Dutch mentality.

Above all things, Hals did use his eyes, but his interests, when they were not purely artistic, were more particularly of a psychological nature. Seldom has a genius of the brush allowed himself to be so captivated by the appearance of the purely material. He devoted the whole of his attention to the human face, the human figure, the clothes of the individual. Everything he came across, in or on the person, he painted. The skin, the hair, the eyes, the hands, and also the fabrics of silk, satin, brocade, bombazine, lace, and the most extravagant ornaments, as well as the drinking glasses in the hands, the beakers and the tobacco pipes. With a delicate brush he even painted brilliant little still lifes of the very meals at which the people were sitting. And then that light over everything. But he never went beyond the immediate surroundings of the sitter.

6

His treatment of the subject remained limited to the posture, the action (a more or less mobile position) to no more than a burst of laughter and sometimes a sort of gallant gesture.

The only slight exceptions to this rule are the singing boys, the jester playing his lute and, of course, the fisher girls and boys who seem to have been snapped photographically as they passed by. No portraits possess more mobility than those by Hals, but no other painter of his time so seldom involved his subjects in dynamic scenes, preferring to depict them in a sort of still life.

Is there an explanation for this fixation on people posing? Probably none other than the obvious one: Frans Hals painted what he was asked to paint. They asked him for that in which these convivial people were most interested: the personal appearance and the distinguishing character of the individual. The considerable advantage to himself, and probably no less his love of ease, caused Hals to keep to what he was asked to do, and for which he was sought after in the circle of family and friends.

Such an apparently simple explanation is confirmed by the difference that so clearly exists between the works he was commissioned to do and those which he painted more or less for the fun of it. This painting "for the fun of it" would keep him with his family or take him from his fireside to a milieu where he could meet with a cheerful, informal company of, say, fisherfolk. Or maybe there is quite a different explanation for those fishermen and those fish-peddling girls? One must never be too positive; perhaps these youngsters were all employed by a herring dealer who wanted to have his employees—perhaps his own children—painted for the adornment of his office. One thing is certain, and that is that Hals led a pretty free and easy social life, and that we can attribute this insouciance to his artistic activities.

He was not a painter whose art produced a solution (temporary, of course) to the mystery of life! He was no methodical genius who canonized his own peculiar style in his paintings. He was not a painter who, like Rembrandt, was mesmerized by his own countenance. And finally, compared with so many others, he was not even a prolific painter. In his *modus operandi* there was a certain impatience; he made no pencil sketches beforehand, but immediately started putting his concepts onto the canvas. He was much more of a genius by dedication, an artistic genius whose vision was limited to avidly depicting the visual realities, to his sympathy for people and his irony towards some of them. For the careful examiner not only perceives this irony in the deadly pictures of the regents, but much earlier in portraits such as that of Willem van Heythuysen, in which Hals paints into the picture just a little too much of the braggadocio for which he was evidently asked; he may even be suspected of a certain suggestion of mockery (p. 33).

The Events of His Life

Frans Hals was born in Antwerp in or about 1580, but went to Haarlem with his parents in his early youth. He was mentioned as a pupil of Karel van Mander, but we can hardly trace any of the latter's influence. The year 1603 must have been the very last year of his apprenticeship, as in that year Van Mander left Haarlem to give up painting and devote himself to literature. The earliest known work by Hals dates from 1611, which means that we have no knowledge of any paintings he may have done before his thirty-first year. That would not appear to be an insurmountable loss when we look at the very unoriginal painting of Zaffius (p. 19). All the same, it is puzzling that it took such a long time for the ability of a man of genius to manifest itself. Without any doubt, however, there must have been good reasons to commission him in 1616 to paint the "Banquet of the Officers of the Civic Guard of St. George, Haarlem" (p. 24). His talent must have been known and acknowledged by that time.

It was in this same year that Hals, who was to travel so little during the rest of his life and who remained so faithful to his

Self-portrait, 1639 (detail of the painting on page 56; second figure from the left, upper row)

home town, journeyed to Antwerp. There he probably visited Rubens. Very little is known about his other contacts with renowned colleagues. We are, however, aware that the famous Anthony van Dyck thought it worth while to pay Hals a visit in Haarlem in 1632. Rubens would also appear to have visited him. This indicates how well known Hals was, a fact which is also to be gathered from the lengthy list of his pupils. This not only includes his sons Frans, Harmen, and Claesz, but also Johannes Verspronck, P. Soutman, Judith Leyster (many of whose works were for a time attributed to Hals himself), Willem Buytewech, Adriaen Brouwer, Adriaen and Isaac van Ostade, Jan Molenaer, and others. And we must not overlook the influence he must also have exercised on those who were not his pupils.

In 1608 Hals married Annetje Hermansdochter, of whom we know only that she bore him two children, died in 1615, and left him a house. Then on February 12, 1617, Hals married Liesbeth Reyniers, just in time for their first child to be born legitimately nine days later. She presented her husband with ten more children, who must certainly have contributed (probably more than the use of alcohol, of which the gossip-writer Houbraken accused him) to keep Hals in financial difficulties all his life. These difficulties caused him a great deal of trouble, but did not prevent him from being able to play a significant part in the life of Haarlem. From 1616 to 1625 he was a member of the Society of Rhetoricians "De Wijn-gaertranken"; later he became an officer of the "Schutters-gilde" (Guild of the Civic Guard). In spite of non-payment of dues he was still on the list of members in 1644, and even in 1661, when he was of great age, he still held the rank of Officer. He was, as a matter of course, also a member of the Guild of St. Luke.

There appears to have been a certain untidiness about his life, though it was not our Frans Hals, as Houbraken falsely stated and Bredius denied, but a namesake who is reputed to have given his first wife such a dreadful beating that she died from the effects. But in 1654 his furniture and his pictures were confiscated to settle a debt—to the baker! In other respects too his life was not always fortunate; he had a son who became insane and a daughter who had an illegitimate child in the workhouse and who, according to more virtuous ladies, had associated with a number of men.

All these blemishes on his respectability did not prevent Hals —probably an exceptionally agreeable fellow to associate with because of his affability and intelligence—from remaining a favourite painter for Haarlem, being consultant to the city on art matters, receiving more commissions than any other artist to paint the official guilds, and enjoying public support in various forms to a very advanced age.

With his commissions from the most important people he could quietly remain in Haarlem; it was considered well worth while to go to him. The time, in 1633, when he had to travel regularly to Amsterdam to paint the group portrait of the Civic Guard of St. Hadrian only brought him misery. He grumbled about having to make the journeys, the expense, his having perforce to hang around in Amsterdam pothouses, and about the honorarium, which was too small because of all this. And although he was constantly being summoned to do the work, he finally declined both the honour and the honorarium, and Pieter Codde completed the canvas.

When he was an old man, in 1662, he received from the city (Haarlem) a stipend of 200 guilders per annum. His rent and his debts were paid, and he was provided with fuel. After his death in 1666 he was buried in the Church of St. Bavo at the city's expense. And why should it be said: "At the expense of the Parish"?

The World of His Art

Most of the two hundred or so paintings that we know to be by Frans Hals are portraits. The other works are genre pieces in which the action involves an isolated human figure painted on a large scale. This holds good for the many fisher boys and girls who carry their baskets as an attribute in an allegory and are very lively and active, but are not actually working and do not together form a tableau such as one can see in the work of his own pupils Brouwer and Van Ostade, who present scenes of taverns, fairs, and wedding parties, in which a lot of men and women are talking and laughing and quarrelling.

The portraitlike conception of Hals' genre is also seen in the very large group paintings of guards. Here one realizes clearly that those men, gesticulating and looking at us, are there in order to have their external appearance painted, and not for the sake of the interesting proceedings with which they were supposed to be occupied. But of course that is understandable; after all, they are there to make as brave a show as possible. In his other genre pictures this is less obvious, and is only to be explained by Hals' preference for the person as character and presence. And that is why he does not portray a person at a time in his activity when he could only show a small facet of his personality, but presents him as a complete entity whose qualities he read from his countenance and from his attitude, and blended them together in the portrait.

Is a portrait, then, only a synthesis, merely an amalgamation of qualities in one situation? We must surely admit that Hals' portraits do have something about them of genre, which, even in his case, is just a shade more bound up with a moment in time. "The Merry Drinker" (p. 61) has been caught as though with a camera. And wherever else someone lifts a glass, strikes a lute, or bursts into laughter, like "The Mulatto" (p. 43), it seems as though he has been caught in the flash of a second. The artist has seized the pulsation of life itself, which has not been halted or stylized into a mere pose for the painter and for the world.

Quite a lot of people had their portraits painted. Hals was not then a painter of world renown, as he is today, but in Haarlem itself, and also elsewhere in Holland, many people came to him to have their portraits done in distinguished attire and prefer-ably in an awe-inspiring posture. Those were the men of

Haarlem—the burgomasters, the regents, the preachers, the tradesmen, and the brewers—sometimes with their wives. And because of the reputation which had put other portrait painters in the shade, there came to Hals famous statesmen from outside Haarlem, theologians, diplomats, and even a philosopher such as Descartes, who then resided in Amsterdam.

This procession of more or less illustrious figures remains ineffaceably in our imagination. No one could forget what a conceited fellow the "Laughing Cavalier" was (p. 27), or the diplomat Massa, who sits posing in the middle of a brilliant conversation (p. 42), or the immense superiority and self-confidence of Paulus van Beresteyn (p. 26), or the ludicrous pose of Willem van Heythuysen propping himself up with his sword (p. 33). Maria Vooght, in her portrait in the Rijksmuseum in Amsterdam, represents the completely noble and righteous Dutch woman of middle age. But who could be otherwise than enchanted by the charm which radiates from Isabella Cooymans toward her husband Stephan Geraerdts (pp. 53, 52)?

Almost all of them remain in our minds as intensely alive persons who must have been well worth meeting. Not so much because they were all so tremendously gifted with ability, but because they appear before us as living persons, keen and sure of themselves; as people who considered life worth living, even though they did not want to dwell too much on the whys and wherefores. That is what they were like, at any rate that is how Hals shows them to us—the same men and women who, when painted by De Keyser, were so lacking in gallantry, by Mierevelt so humourlessly serious, by Van der Helst so noisily insignificant—but by Rembrandt so moving.

Hals' style of painting ensured that most of his sitters were given their just due and sometimes more. Only a few portraits fell short of the mark, because Hals depicted nothing but that unusual directness with which, by turns, many human qualities show to full advantage: contentedness, openheartedness, kindness, rectitude, seriousness, frivolity, melancholy. But

13

sometimes one sees no more than a fraction of these inborn or acquired qualities, only a laugh, a friendly feeling, amusement, or physical satisfaction. Such passing psychical situations can make splendid illustrations of life, but a person who is only observed at such a fleeting moment naturally gets less than his due. An artist who works in such fashion does indeed paint, according to the excellent words of Martin, "without spiritual pause".

However, who is going to regret that the man who was "The Merry Drinker" has been completely forgotten as a spiritual creature, when we can see so clearly with our own eyes both the drinking and the pleasure of it being enjoyed by this somewhat uninteresting, rich, and slovenly dressed fellow? It is only in a portrait of Descartes that one perceives the limits of Hals' ability. We see a splendidly painted, very remarkable head, which reveals just a shade too little of the genius of the subject and too much of the skill of the painter in this brilliant record of the celebrated man (p. 51).

What remains most clearly in our memory is the immediate closeness of the many Dutch characters, of which Hals has not only shown us the qualities, but above all the actual mode of life of his sitters, and has managed also to convey as much movement as is possible to a subject standing or sitting still. Therefore we often see a smile round the lips and a very direct gaze at us, both of which clearly suggest movement in time. Sometimes this suggestion of movement is still more striking because the figures are placed as though turning around, as in the portrait of Massa (p. 42), in which he is sitting turned towards his right and is looking to our left. Movement is even more strongly indicated when a hand is holding a glass or making a gesture. They are all accents which bring a definite sense of movement into a portrait. But even though these motions have nothing to do with the tormented movements of mannerist compositions, they are all the same connected quite definitely with the European trend of those times, and that is why this style of portraiture clearly signifies the introduction of the baroque style into the Netherlands, which used to arrange its models so trimly and so stiffly. It is from this baroque style that the portraits of Hals derived the liveliness, the turning of the head and of the figure, the contact with the world outside the actual painting. And that is why his subjects laugh, as those of Velázquez often do, so that their feelings spread over their faces. In order to bring the exterior movement into contact with the inner feelings. And to enable the painting to play upon human emotions.

One other thing should be pointed out here about this "immediate closeness" mentioned above. Of course this is in part an illusion, but on the other hand it is also a fact. In order to illustrate the instantaneous quality of Hals' works, we could use a term from photography and speak of his "close-ups", indicating how he draws his personages right up to the front of the painting, and makes our eyes wander over broadly observed details which he has, as it were, sliced out of reality. That also creates movement, the movement of the observant person walking through life who not only sees things in their broad context, in well-considered compositions, but also has an eye for things close by that fascinate him.

His Works

Some of Frans Hals' works are dated, and others we can, with certainty or with some hesitation, place in chronological order. We do not know of many paintings of his early days, though the portrait of Zaffius (p. 19) does belong to that period. The priest has a keen enough look, but the portrait has no brilliance whatever, no movement, no sparkle. Another early work, "Nurse and Child" (p. 21), shows much greater maturity, but along with the captivating naturalness of the facial expression we still notice a stiffness in the pose and a thoughtfulness in the gesture, which give the picture a kind of double quality of self-conscious artlessness. Possessed of great possibilities—perhaps the gaze of the woman and the little child

15

surprises us still more than the rendering of the rich attire—the portrait has the qualities that the nurse herself shows; it is a talented, but also a diffident picture.

Ease of movement is to be seen for the first time, surprisingly, in the portrait group of "The Civic Guard of St. George", painted in 1616. If we start judging the situation logically, there is artificiality enough in this picture (pp. 23-25). We notice that apparently it is possible simultaneously to hold an animated conversation, to preside over and extol the banquet at a table which is too small, to show the colours and to so stare at the onlooker that the central figure in the foreground turns his broad head around, and, somewhat more laboriously, his heavy body too. It is a composition which is not at all concerned with the appropriateness of a situation, but much rather with showing clearly who are present, what they look lik—burly, well-fed men of Holland; what they represent—the officers of the civic guard; what they are engaged upon—the meal, which is a banquet, and, to judge by their figures, must also be a frequent pastime against the boredom of not very intellectual people.

In this respect the liveliness is indeed bewildering, and the baroque movement is brilliantly introduced into the composition. The three figures at the left form the beginning of the diagonal which extends through the figure of the flag-bearer and the flag he is carrying; in the picture he is actually turning in this complicated posture. The landscape gives depth to the painting, while the unknown figure in the foreground and also the gesturing gentleman who turns himself completely towards us bring the whole retinue of men who belong to them to the forefront, toward us, the spectators. The figure sitting to the left and the one standing on the right enclose the composition: the carver seems, in spite of his occupation, to be, psychologically, the central figure of the hierarchy, while above, to the left, a large drapery provides abstract movement to symbolize the phase of the baroque style which dominates this painting.

16

In 1627 Frans Hals painted "Banquet of the Officers of the Civic Guard of St. Hadrian" (pp. 28, 29). In this painting we see a liveliness which could justifiably be described as "tumult", contained within a tight, almost scholastic, composition of crosswise diagonals. To the left a large standing figure balances the composition; to the right, it is somewhat more open than in the previously mentioned picture. But greater symmetry in an ensemble of figures is hardly conceivable, when we look at the men sitting back to back in the foreground. Yet here again this orderliness is the necessary counterpoise to the commotion taking place because everyone is busy with everything at the same time. One is showing off his attire; another is holding a quill pen in order to indicate his work as secretary. A third is only interested in having his empty wine glass filled, and yet another appears to be ogling us to seek our approval.

Dated the same year (1627) there is another "Banquet of the Civic Guard of St. George" (pp. 22, 30). There again we see orderliness, but it is more self-evident, more tranquil, and the group is composed with greater ingenuity. Everyone has availed himself very frankly of the opportunity to be in the picture, and the hierarchy of the officers differing in rank and occupation seems to have been less strictly taken into account. The lowest in rank actually plays the chief role in the picture. The men converse, drink, and eat just as cheerfully as in the previous paintings, but here we find more cohesion, and attention to the food is somewhat less obtrusively demanded by that bowl of oysters over which the head of the table is squeezing a lemon. Nicholaes de Wael wants it to be known that his glass is empty, but any coarseness is removed from the gesture by its elegance.

Just as the demands of composition take precedence over considerations of official rank, the painter's art reigns supreme in the whole of this work. The little groups and the individuals are not only placed in a better seating arrangement, but they have been benevolently subordinated to the light that is carefully but sensitively distributed over the figures, modelling them plastically and still binding them all in one source of light. It is not only the people but particularly the objects in the picture that create magnificent high lights: that play of white collars is so fascinating; the sleeve of De Wael is thrust forward so matchlessly, and Hals has exercised his pure artistic skill so lyrically with De Wael's cloak, with the suit of the flag-bearer, and with the sleeve of the man drinking on the left.

The "Meeting of the Officers and Subalterns of the Civic Guard of St. Hadrian", of 1633 (p. 35), astonishes us by its startling rendering of fabrics and colours and by the most splendid portraits, of which that of the Commandant is most striking; the rest of the scene is lively, but does not strike one as a good composition—in fact, we are rather disturbed by the fact that it falls into two parts.

Although the "Officers and Subalterns of the Civic Guard of St. George", of 1639 (pp. 56, 57), seems at first sight to contain a reversion to a former, more forced, arrangement of the group, this composition of Hals is really much more variegated, with its careful division in the middle by the golden figure of the Captain in his baroque attitude. The colours and the positions of the officers also make for variation. The non-commissioned officers above form a surprising sort of gallery. Frans Hals brought about the apotheosis of the so-called "Civic Guard" group-paintings, which since the second quarter of the sixteenth century were almost never met with outside Holland. Only the "Night Watch" of Rembrandt makes us temporarily forget these works.

There are a few group portraits by Frans Hals apart from those of the guardsmen and regents, such as the family groups, of which I want to mention the "Young Married Couple" (p. 31). They are sitting in the open air, in an extremely friendly and affectionate attitude, with an architectural fantasy in the background, and, in the foreground, plants symbolical of conjugal fidelity and male and female qualities. This picture seems, for Hals, the acme of spatiality, nature, architecture, and sym-

18 (continued on page 73)

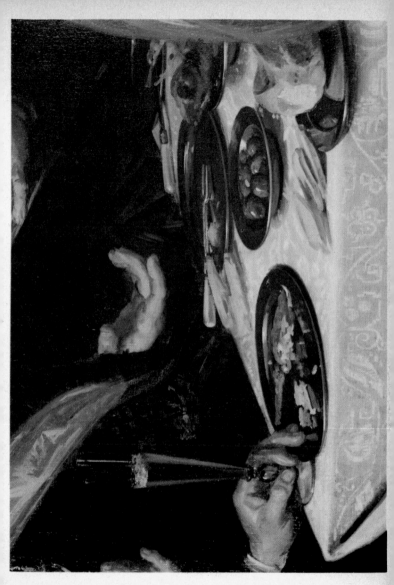

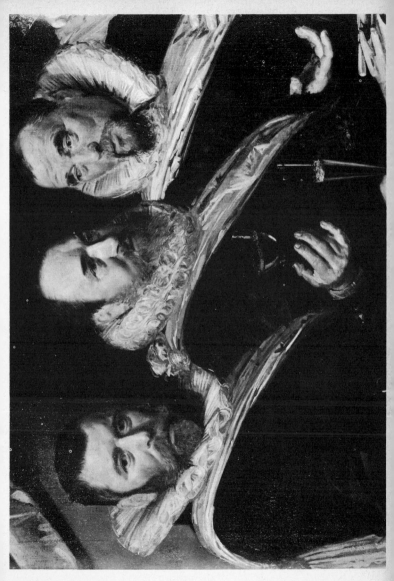

51

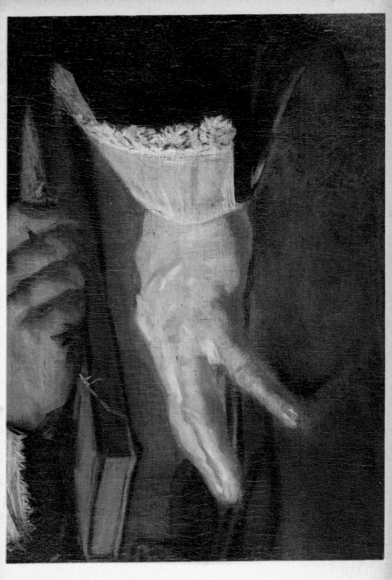

65

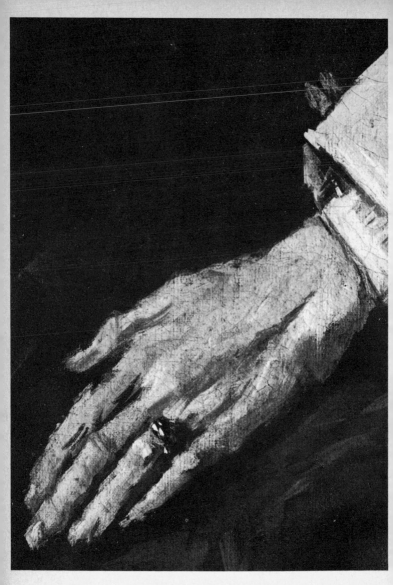

bolism. Still, it was tradition—and the man who gave him the commission—who were really responsible for it.

The antithesis of this tranquil, loving couple would seem to be "Yonker Ramp and His Sweetheart" (p. 32). Without meeting here with frivolity, the atmosphere is totally different, overflowing with exuberance, and completely in keeping with the bohemian branch of Hals' models.

A rather outstanding painting in the work of Frans Hals is that of the "Regents (Governors) of the St. Elizabeth Hospital in Haarlem" (pp. 62, 63). The gentlemen are sitting silently together, mesmerized by the eyes of the painter. They are abundantly lighted by the strong sunlight coming through a high window. There is a genial and very dignified atmosphere. Though the composition is very explicit—four heads in one line, three in a triangle—an emphatic rhythm of hats, collars, and hands—there is all the same a definite accent on the chairman, who sits turned to the left; especially because the light falls on him in particular, on his resolute hand and on his face, which, by his friendly expression and his smile, is noteworthy among the impassive countenances of the others. It is a painting which has a calmer effect than much of Hals' work, somewhat tamer than the pictures of the guards, and less detailed as far as the persons are concerned. Abstract compositional values play the chief part; it is to a high degree an artistic unity of colour, light, line, modelling and atmosphere.

Most of Hals' work consists of portraits which are naturally distinguished by the characters they portray, of which we have already noted the general characteristics above. The pose of the sitter is either a standing or a sitting one, seldom fulllength, right in the forefront at the edge of the frame, against a lighter background upon which the family coat of arms is sometimes painted in miniature. On rare occasions there was an exception to this, as in the Lichtenstein portrait of Willem van Heythuysen (p. 33), who stands full-length in front of and under a baroque drapery. Very diverse personages are portrayed, and almost always Hals subordinated himself

73

to the sitter, though his respect, his interest, and sometimes his irony can be sensed.

In addition to the extensive series of commissioned portraits, there were other portraits which form a separate category: those of the fishermen's boys and girls, of which the authenticity of many is doubtful, though a few undoubtedly were executed by Frans Hals in spite of their not being quite in keeping with the majority of his works. However lively the commissioned portraits may be, their purpose is always to face towards the onlooker, and they even possess the excellent quality of achieving that direct and perceptible bond. The portraits of the fishermen's children and similar ones give the impression of an event which the onlooker may be able to see in close proximity, but to which, nevertheless, he is not a party. No communication between the onlooker and the subject of the picture is possible. There was no time for posing —indeed, barely time to do the actual painting. For Hals, who always had a flowing and carefree brush, painted these portraits very vigorously indeed, almost as quickly as the rapidity of movement being recorded—like a fisherman tilting a mug of beer, or a girl who smilingly offers her basket of fish.

The result of sketchy brushstrokes has never shown a more ruffled effect, but the impressionistic effect was quite obviously intentional, expecially when one examines the backgrounds of high and wildly dashing waves, rippled sand dunes, agitated skies, and tumbling birds. These girls and boys are, as we say, "taken from life", that is shown during their work. They are quite aware that they are being painted, but their laugh seems to be one of apology for having been caught doing their jobs (p. 45).

"The Bohemian Girl", in the Louvre (p. 60), acts purely with her eyes and with a few other pleasant attributes and qualities, but she again has that powerful directness and an interest for someone other than the onlooker. Just as the "Jester" (p. 41) is only interested in his playing and is completely wrapped up in it, and at best looks at the person for whom he is playing.

74

We are in any case outsiders, though nothing escapes us. There are borderline cases in the portraits that are so clearly "genre" —pictures of one single person—such as "The Merry Drinker" (p. 61) and "The Mulatto" (p. 43), who are not in a position to be taken absolutely seriously as individuals and who are so very active that we must regard them as genre. But in these pictures there is very definitely a direct contact with the on-looker. They are the variants on a few details from the pictures of the guards and the regents, where even the most obviously studied pose alternates with a contact between the picture and us onlookers.

Still more direct, if that be possible, are the small circular paintings of children, in which the movement of life has given these pictures immortality (p. 40). The razorlike close-ups and astounding extracts of spontaneous life are brilliantly rendered. Every feature seems to have been directly transferred, and the exuberant atmosphere helps to accentuate the vivacious-ness of the portraits.

Entirely different in conception is another series of portraits of youngsters. These show more thoughtfulness, the gestures are theatrical, and the eye of the painter is more deliberate. Take, for instance, the "Young Man with a Skull" and the "Two Singing Boys" (pp. 38, 39). Such pictures appear to be far more deliberately studied and planned. The fairly ordinary boy's head of the so-called "Hamlet" goes well in a scene of lyrical quality, rendered with a certain degree of pathos: the charm of the young face under the beret with the extravagant feather; the broad, dignified, horizontal folds which give grandeur to the mantle; the outstretched hand which empha-sizes the rhetoric; the death's-head echoing the young counten-ance. Then, of course, as a dominant factor, there is that light, which, here again, sharply defines the chiaroscuro and drama-tizes the whole scene, fitfully illuminating both head and skull, glowing upon the fingers and shining from the background. And if finally we do not forget the actual story—and who could do so now that everything has been so emphatically presented?—only then do we realize properly that, whether it is a question of a dressing-up scene, a play—*Hamlet*—or just pure fantasy, here there is in any case something of the theatre, and of a conscious and considered attitude.

There is drama in the treatment of the lighting and in the conception of the pose; there are also more or less conventional gestures, the meaning of which sets us no problems. Above all, there is a great deal of lyric character in these paintings. The glorification of conscious, experienced beauty. In most of Hals' works we find no trace of such deliberation and elegance. Is this another facet of Frans Hals? It had undoubtedly been one of his preferences, but that was in a period when he had not yet quite found himself. For something like this conception in the art of painting was already known. We can recognize it in the works of the Utrecht painters whom we call Caravaggists: Honthorst, Terbrugghen and others, who were greatly inspired by Italian art, especially by the nobility, the lyrical qualities, the showy chiaroscuro of Caravaggio and his theatrical compositions. Those Utrecht artists represent yet another facet of the middle-class seventeenth century in Holland, and except for Rembrandt, no one ignored them, neither Vermeer nor Frans Hals.

Do the later portraits by Hals need another quality than those of his middle period, and do they sometimes have a different character? We can point to his technique, which was then controlled with inimitable facility, with such lightninglike accuracy that even the "intention" of a sort of impressionism seems to have been lost; so rarely did the brushstrokes run into each other, even when seen from a distance. We get a strong impression that the effect of those dashing, quick, sharp touches of the brush has been sought after for itself alone, as an abstract demonstration of the artist's skill. In my own opinion, a psychological change is also to be found in those later pictures. We meet with less obtrusiveness of the person and of the attire, and find a more tranquil look in the eyes. That calm is not always the same; it can be friendly, interested, and wise, but also superior and resigned, as in the portrait of Oosdorp (p. 67). And we also come upon the amusement which, in some of his pictures, seems to cock a snook at human affairs and is consciously seeking the ludicrous (p. 66). At times Hals paints more mercilessly and becomes satirical. The apotheosis of that style of his took shape in his pictures of the regents and regentesses of the Old Men's Almshouse in Haarlem, in which realism develops into deadly irony.

When Hals painted the "Regents of the Old Men's Almshouse, Haarlem" (pp. 64-65), he was eighty-two. I do not know what the thoughts of an old man are, but probably the nearness of death does away with limits and hindrances. This can have various results. The relativity of human existence can dull the edge of one's judgment, as has frequently been seen. It is also possible that one keeps the same fettered spirit within a decaying body, and then sometimes one plays and over-acts the old man for the sake of his environment, but the man himself is tormented. That is what the greatest writers tell us. In the case of Hals it is evident that old age swept away the hindrances. He always did possess an exceptionally good eye, but he used it with a benevolence which in his mature years completely associated itself with the aggressive good health of his subjects. When he was middle-aged, he communicated to us something of the respect he felt for his dignified and resolute subjects, though he also knew only too well how to depict the extravagant aristocracy, as he did in the portrait of Schade van Westrum (p. 50). Old age may perhaps have affected his out-look, but he was certainly able to interpret his subjects, though in a different way. He had earned the liberty not to have to worry any more about the consequences of his courage; there can be very little to alter in the external circumstances of an old man, supported materially by the welfare services of his city. He availed himself of this freedom to paint his portraits so that his models were not spared in any respect. With the excep-tion of the good-natured father who shares with Hals an understanding about the group of by no means handsome specimens—the Regents, p. 64—there is only the man behind the table who seems to have anything normal about him. The Treasurer has only a mask for a face, and the other three appear to have been failures as human beings. The figure on the left is possessed by insanity, the one on the right is a tall, degenerate lout, and one figure is a bleary-eyed drunkard, characterized by that ludicrous crooked hat on his head. If ever Hals wanted to show the odiousness of slovenliness, he did it here. Fromentin called that nonchalance a questionable example for young painters. But when a painting is something more than merely a pedagogic lesson, no one gets annoyed for a single second because of these wanton, random touches which are, in part, appropriate to a subject conceived in this manner, namely these seedy-looking scallywags with their straight, unwashed hair, their degenerate faces, and the absurdity of their "eloquent" gestures.

We may feel pity for the regents. We are only prejudiced against the regentesses (pp. 68–72) because their pose of righteousness seems convincing. The woman who strikes us as the most lugubrious of them all is the one behind the table with her hollow eye sockets and her clenched fists. The begging Treasurer only strikes us by her merciless friendliness.

The frivolous lady standing up reflects her own stupidity, and the one on the right sitting at the table, with the fever of wickedness on her cheeks and her hand resembling a large knife, also does not require any comment. Here again it is the Mother who, behind her dignity and her genuine rectitude, shows the human virtues of kindliness and simplicity. This canvas has been more carefully painted than that of the regents, and it is just as independent a work of art. The red on the cheeks of one of the women suggests a burning fever, and the book on the table with its yellow parchment and red on the edges is an artistic summing-up by the painter of what has been elaborated psychologically around it.

The reason why the works of Frans Hals make such an over-whelming impression of authenticity is in no small measure due to his method and his technique. His pictures did not grow from rough sketches to careful drawings and then to finished paintings. There are no drawings that can with certainty be ascribed to him, and we know how he sketched in paint directly on the canvas. Anything thought out in advance, theoretical, was alien to his nature, and we must call his method rather one of spontaneity, inventiveness, and improvisation.

His technique is of course closely bound up with his method. The technique most true to life was the one Da Vinci invented called "*sfumato*", by which richly variegated effects were obtained by imposing many transparent paintings over a basic picture. The result of this careful time-consuming technique is an elaborate product in which the comparative velvety authenticity suffered by the loss of a certain spontaneity. Frans Hals, in an extremely personal fashion, anticipated the modern system of painting in wet paint, which makes possible a much quicker method of painting. It is characteristic of the nineteenth-century impressionists that they were the first who, after a relative indifference in the previous years, enthusiastically rediscovered Hals and admired him for his technique.

It is a technique of large, loose strokes of paint, of loosely applied brushstrokes. These brushstrokes conjure up the objects as impressions; it is the brushstrokes that do it. It was not necessary to evoke plastic modelling by painfully painting in light, shadows, and contours. By placing the brushstrokes next to and across each other with various, sometimes strongly contrasting, colours, the light is created, without having to superimpose high lights on other colours. We can see this extremely well in the hands, where the light accents are not applied over ground colours, but are suggested by, for instance, the placing of a strong yellow next to, say, a subdued pink (p. 63).

79

Hals was, especially in his early days, a painter of light. Some of his "Civic Guard" pictures are entirely illuminated by outside light. This also the impressionists admired in him, and in part learned from him. In an entirely new manner he had linked up that light with his skill as a painter. He conjured it up by making its quality, strength, and intensity that of the paint itself. In the "Civic Guard" picture of 1627 (p. 30) he distributes the light harmoniously over the whole scene. In the "Regents of the St. Elizabeth Hospital, Haarlem" (p. 62) he causes it dramatically to determine the scene by letting it shine in spots for emphasis, and bind the parts together by means of the strong tonalities.

In his portraits, lighting does play a prominent part, but its structure is not startling: it always falls from the left, it is clearly a falling light, it throws shadows on faces and clothing, and creates shadows behind the figures, and thus creates space around the figures, which generally either stand or sit against a light abstract background.

The autonomous use of the brushstroke can also be detected in the lace collars and sleeves, which Hals often painted with so much pleasure. Originally he used to devote extreme care to them. Later on, he included these also in his technique of loose brushstrokes. This is clearly to be seen in the portraits of Malle Babbe and Schade van Westrum, to mention two extremes (pp. 59, 50). Babbe's collar has been loosely swept together, just as the short collar of the pedantic lawyer has been. And his silken sleeve is built up of darting brushstrokes. It is characteristic of these and of most of the other brushstrokes that they shoot sharply over the plane in zigzagging barbed hooks. Quickly applied, frayed in shape.

Towards the end of his life, he ventured to carry his technical improvisations much further. With what a masterly touch, light and transparent, and with what unparalleled daring, did Hals then paint is nowhere better demonstrated than in the painting of the regentesses, where the coquettish standing woman sticks her sheeplike head above a collar that looks as light as a butterfly, almost transparent, and yet is painted with a few broad brushstrokes (p. 69). It is one of the details in the work in which everyone forgets the subject of the picture in admiration of the genius of the painter, of the creation of a blossoming white plane.

In the technique of Frans Hals we can trace a gradual evolution, over the years, towards still more fluency, more independence in style, and a more facile use of a difficult technique. His evolution in use of colours is much more evident. At first his colouring was very eloquently and festively variegated. In later years his palette became soberer and lighter, until in his forties he leaned towards greys and blacks. This development ran parallel with the trend in fashion from gay colours to a respectable black. Perhaps this trend just happened to run parallel to his own state of mind, which developed from boisterousness to a mature tranquillity, to end with a supremely personal outlook, which made the world subservient to those spectral images in black, red, and grey, the products of his genius.

The Judgment of Time

When we formulate our opinion on the work of Frans Hals we do so not without listening curiously to what people of other times have said about him and his art. They indicate to us, as it were, the "possibilities" that were hidden in him. Our century notices things which eluded a former one, and, on the other hand, we are but little interested in qualities which excited a former generation. That over-stressing of certain facets in various periods is the accent of a particular life-style, but at the same time it does give us the description of the components of genius.

The seventeenth century itself passed judgment upon Hals. That judgment was primarily expressed by the many commissions for portraits which the master received. He did also paint many very ordinary people, and, with apparent sympathy, those who were on the fringe of decent society. The majority of his models however, were prosperous burghers, and even aristocrats and scholars. At the end of Hals' life tastes changed, and preference was given to more flattering portraits with more classical pretensions, but his fame remained intact. There is always something scandalous in the scanty rewards the community pays for artistic work, but the payment to Frans Hals of a small stipend in his old age—and even those insulting three wagons of peat—still shows, in all its shabbiness, a certain token of appreciation. In Holland, where art possessed no aura of godliness, where people were very commercial-minded, and where they did not aspire to a higher spiritual plane, they did uphold what was honourable in society.

The first art histories honour the artist, but slander the man. Like Arnold Houbraken, who, in his "Great Theatre of Netherlands Painters", pictured Hals as a drunkard and a knave, but whose sensational account in 1718 was not authentic and has been contradicted in many details.

It stands to reason that Hals could not have become the fêted artist of the shallow and elegant-mannered eighteenth century. But even in those years he was not forgotten; this is indicated most of all by the fairly frequent reproductions of his works by graphic artists. Often there remained but little of his brilliant technique, but it was made pretty clear that both his skill in portraiture and his exuberant spirits had been recognized and appreciated.

One of the most remakable expressions of appreciation in the nineteenth century I consider to be the copying of "Malle Babbe" by Courbet, who called this painting the most beautiful in the world. It was an appreciation *avant la lettre* when we bear in mind the subsequent veneration of Hals by the impressionists. We can also definitely deduce what a man like Courbet could appreciate from his own point of view, and this was beyond doubt the drastic, robust artist's style and Hals' relentless realism. It was, it appears, respect for the purest painting, and for the keenness of eye which overlooked nothing.

The impressionists have perhaps appreciated and praised Hals' technique in greater measure; in 1872 Manet journeyed to Haarlem to study this technique. In the works of Hals they were able to find what they themselves sought and put into practice: a palette of rhythmic and freely applied brush-strokes. They were able to see there the unblended strokes of paint, which the eye brought together, and from which it derived the greatest possible impression of life. They also saw what had escaped Fromentin, namely, that there was no question at all of slovenliness. In his *Maîtres d'autrefois* (*Masters of the Olden Times*) (1876), he wrote: "At the moment the name of Hals is mentioned again in our school of painting, now that the taste for naturalness is returning with some sensationalism and no less exaggeration. His technique serves as a programme for certain trends, according to which, unfortunately, the most pedestrian exactitude is accepted as the truth, and the greatest possible carelessness for the last word in knowledge and good taste". And he asked why, with all Hals' great qualities, only his faults should be extolled.

He does not mention anything of what, later on, intrigued the all too-literary Claudel so greatly: the drama of the late paintings. Claudel also made a precise psychological differentiation between the "Civic Guards" pictures: "overgrown boys amusing themselves", and the later "Regents" pictures, about which he says: "Neither in Goya nor in El Greco do we find anything so masterly, anything so frightful, for Hell itself is less forbidding for us than limbo." Claudel does not forget form and colour as he writes figuratively about "that book of which the reflection has the shine of bones, and which on the edge is as red as glowing coals", and he considers the artist's style not only as regards quality but also in relation to psyche and sentiments and erudition. That is why he sees in the women the decay of the flesh and—if that were possible—the soul. And that is why he speaks of the "regents" as the "noblemen from the other side of the grave".

Van Gogh's esteem for Hals is also noteworthy. He would be

83

inclined to give a more profound meaning to the portrait, but next to psychology and human greatness, pure painting interested him most. And so, both for psychological reasons and for his painting style, Van Gogh admired Frans Hals. He could characterize the landlady of an inn as a pretty girl "lively and piquant à la Frans Hals". In 1885 he studied Hals and appreciated him especially because of his use of colour, saying: "In short, Frans Hals is a colourist like Veronese, like Rubens, like Delacroix, like Velázquez."

André Malraux interprets somewhat more freely—and I think more correctly—when he asks: "What was Hals after when he painted the regents? Psychological expression? Let us stop confusing the examination of character with the hate which motivates this vengeful art of painting; what he is after is a canvas to kill all other canvases, and first of all his own!" They are works of vengeance and they avenge themselves upon a flaunting, ridiculous world which out of benevolence towards him sits down and compels him to become immortal. In these pictures Hals reaches the autonomous world in which he rules as an artist and establishes his truth. He makes the regents into servants of his vision. He painted the likeness of his own genius. Those who granted him commissions share in the end the mighty favours of Hals, constituted by his paintings. And though painting is not just the handling of paint, but also the utilization of a number of universal human qualities from intelligence to sensitivity, from cold cerebration to religious awe, these qualities cannot find expression without that power of painting. Today we realize this even more clearly than Malraux, whose outlook on modern art in 1947-50 was still greatly influenced by expressionism and cubism. Perhaps through the most modern currents we have learned to understand better that ability to conjure up reality by means of spots, strokes, and dots. Is that what Fromentin also experienced as a "mighty abstraction" but found completely insufficient? It is that which strikes the untrained person less forcibly, but which makes the essence of the painting—in fact, it *is* the painting.

Through the art of painting, and through its plastic means, we are able to say what we see. It is that independent brushstroke —that "painter's handwriting"—which makes the network of paints in which both the visual reality and our human feelings are intertwined. In the old-fashioned way, we can say that Frans Hals was completely master of this art of painting. But every epoch makes its own history out of the past. The nineteenth-century impressionists recognized Hals as an exemplary and enlightened impressionist. It constitutes our own distinction that even with this painter who was so earthy, and seemed to present little more than stark reality, we also have discovered in his art that autonomous handwriting as his prime quality. With Frans Hals the persons become more impressive as that handwriting becomes more striking and more uninhibited, a handwriting in which the wind of inspiration seems to have directed the paint brushes—we see therein such breakneck speed and so much apparent arbitrariness.

LIST OF ILLUSTRATIONS

Page

44 GENTLEMAN WITH GLOVES
1639; $33\frac{1}{8}\times26\frac{1}{2}$ in.; Ermitage, Leningrad

45 FISHER BOY
About 1627-30; $31\frac{1}{2}\times23\frac{3}{4}$ in.; Collection Fürst zu Bentheim und Steinfurt, Burgsteinfurt

46 GENTLEMAN STANDING
About 1643; $45\frac{1}{4}\times33\frac{1}{2}$ in.; National Gallery, Edinburgh

47 MRS. BODOLPHE
1643; $48\frac{1}{2}\times38\frac{1}{2}$ in.; Yale University Art Gallery (bequest of Stephen Carlton Clark), New Haven, Connecticut

48 JOHANNES HOORNBEEK
1645; $31\frac{1}{4}\times26\frac{3}{4}$ in.; Royal Museum of Fine Arts, Brussels

49 BALTHASAR COYMANS
1645; $29\frac{1}{8}\times24\frac{1}{2}$ in.; National Gallery of Art (A. W. Mellon collection), Washington

50 JASPER SCHADE VAN WESTRUM
1645; $31\frac{1}{2}\times26\frac{1}{2}$ in.; National Museum, Prague

51 RENÉ DESCARTES
About 1649; $7\frac{1}{2}\times5\frac{1}{2}$ in.; National Art Museum, Copenhagen

52 STEPHANUS GERAERDTS
1650-52; $45\frac{1}{2}\times34\frac{1}{2}$ in.; Royal Museum of Fine Arts, Antwerp

53 ISABELLA COYMANS (WIFE OF STEPHANUS GERAERDTS)
1650-52; $45\frac{3}{4}\times33\frac{7}{8}$ in.; private collection

54 PORTRAIT OF A GENTLEMAN
1652; $24\frac{3}{8}\times18\frac{1}{4}$ in.; Museum of Fine Arts, Budapest

55 GENTLEMAN STANDING
1635; $48\frac{5}{8}\times37\frac{1}{2}$ in.; Boymans-van Beuningen Museum, Rotterdam

56 OFFICERS AND SUBALTERNS OF THE CIVIC GUARD OF ST. GEORGE, HAARLEM
1639; $81\frac{3}{4}\times165\frac{1}{4}$ in.; Frans Hals Museum, Haarlem